# Sum... of

MW00930210

# The Plot to Destroy Democracy

## Malcolm Nance

*Conversation Starters*

# By BookHabits

# Bonus Downloads
*Get Free Books with **Any Purchase** of* Conversation Starters!

Every purchase comes with a FREE download!

*Add spice to any conversation*
*Never run out of things to say*
*Spend time with those you love*

**Get it Now**

or Click Here.

**Scan Your Phone**

## Tips for Using Conversation Starters:

EVERY GOOD BOOK CONTAINS A WORLD FAR DEEPER THAN the surface of its pages. Questions herein are designed to bring us beneath the surface of the page and invite us into the world that lives on. These questions can be used to:

- Foster a deeper understanding of the book
- Promote an atmosphere of discussion for groups
- Assist in the study of the book, either individually or corporately
- Explore unseen realms of the book as never seen before

# Table of Contents

# Introducing *The Plot to Destroy Democracy*

**M**ALCOLM NANCE IS A FAMILIAR VOICE IN counterterrorism and intelligence. He is NBC's counterterrorism analyst and he has authored two books in 2016 - *Defeating ISIS: Who They Are, How They Fight, What They Believe* and *The Plot to Hack America.* Malcolm Nance is a former United States Navy senior petty officer. He is a specialist in Navy Cryptology. During his thirty-five years of service in the U.S. Navy, he was involved in numerous counter-terrorism, intelligence and combat operations.

His newest non-fiction book is *The Plot to Destroy Democracy: How Putin and His Spies Are Undermining America and Dismantling the West.* In his newest non-fiction, Nance discloses the covert operations behind the 2016 U.S. elections. He exposes how Vladimir Putin and his spy agencies used blackmail, espionage, assassination, and psychological warfare during the elections. Nance writes a rehash of the Russian government's plot to hack into voter databases, Democratic officials' emails and social media to flood pro-Trump fake news. Nance also exposes the Trump's senior staff and family had suspicious meetings during the 2016 U.S. presidential election.

NATO, the European Union and the collective western democracy is at threat because of Putin's plot. In this comprehensive exposé, Nance utilized top-secret Russian-sourced political and hybrid warfare strategy documents. Apparently, Putin's grand plan to undermine American institutions began during the Cold War and still continues to this day. Nance employs comprehensive and original research together with interviews with experts in espionage. According to Nance, the hacking of the recent U.S. elections is the first step to the destabilization of the West for Russia. He argues that Putin's Russian enmity has revived his second term as president. He has turned Kopromat and other active measures, including KGB training, to exploit the existing divisions within the American government.

Since 1945, Russia and his fifth column allies have been manipulating elections in order to reengineer the political landscape of the free world. This manipulation comes in many forms – cyberwarfare, political propaganda, perception manipulation of the public through American news, traditional media, social media and the internet. These tactics will be used again and again to break institutions apart until democracy is unrecognizable. Nance has been summoned by the Congress, the House of Representatives and Senate Intelligence Committee to testify about the details of the election manipulation. The administration calls Nance's allegation a misperception and accident. Nance counters that "coincidence takes a lot of planning."

In his book, he reveals how Donald Trump has been suported by Russia. Putin has supported not only Trump's campaigns but also the campaigns of right-wing extremists throughout U.S. and Europe. Since 2010, Putin has been working with his agencies to convert democratic institutions into authoritarian ethnonationalist regimes through the leverage an "axis of autocracy" and Donald Trump's victory in the 2016 elections.

With the victory of Trump comes Vladimir Putin's access to U.S. power. Nance calls Russian president Vladimir Putin "the first Russian president of the United States." He claims that this electoral victory was no less "won with the aid of Americans who had turned on their own values." With this perspective, everyone is implicated – from the pro-Trump voters who casted their ballots to liberal media and its obsession with Clinton's emails.

Nance argues in his detailed work of conspiracy theory that Putin is bent on world domination and America's current president Donald Trump is just his puppet. According to Nance, Trump is a narcissist whose idiocy aids Putin to pull America down. He writes that Trump is doing so for monetary gain along with "the American Goebbels" - Republicans, white nationalists, and former Breitbart News executive chairman turned presidential advisor Steve Bannon. Nance argues that much of the planning were done by the Kremlin and executed by Steve Brannon as he is a key person in forging America into a pro-Moscow conservative movement. The author concludes his arguments and rests his case with a provocative declaration that will spawn even more divisions all on its own: "Trump has definitely convinced me that he transitioned from an unwitting asset of Vladimir Putin to a willing asset working in league with the Russian Federation."

*Net Galley* describes Malcolm Nance's *The Plot to Destroy Democracy: How Putin and His Spies Are Undermining America and Dismantling the West* "revelatory, insightful and shocking." *Kirkus Reviews* says that Nance's book "convincing and alarming." *Publishers Weekly* was hard to convince. They depict Nance's book as an "unconvincing exaggeration of genuine misconduct into cartoonish supervillainy". Malcolm Nance's newest non-fiction will be hit the bookshelves on June 2018.

# Discussion Questions

*"Get Ready to Enter a New World"*

**Tip:** Begin with questions dealing with broader issues to ensure ample time for quality discussions. Read through all discussion questions before engaging.

~~~

## question 1

Trump's campaign figures and family had suspicious meetings with Russian authorities during the campaign. According to Nance, who is the key person in forging America into a pro-Moscow movement?

~~~

## question 2

Putin's grand plan to undermine American institutions began during the Cold War and still continues to this day. What instances has Nance cited that proves Russian's plans that have been in effect since the Cold War?

## question 3

Nance calls Russian president Vladimir Putin "the first Russian president of the United States." Why does he call him so? Why is Putin as victorious when Trump won the elections?

~ ~ ~

~~~

## question 4

During the electoral campaign in 2016, Trump's campaign officials and family had suspicious meetings with Russian authorities. Who among Trump's camp were seen in these meetings?

~~~

## question 5

Since 2010, Putin has been working with his agencies to bring Trump into the 2016 presidential elections. What are the evidences Nance presented to strengthen this claim?

~~~

## question 6

Nance claims that Putin's government seeks to convert American democratic institutions into authoritarian ethnonationalist regimes through the leverage an "axis of autocracy." Describe what is the "axis of autocracy." How does Putin plan on turning democracy into authoritarian regimes?

~~~

## question 7

According to Malcolm Nance, the goal of Putin's government  is to convert American democratic institutions into authoritarian. What will America look like once Putin's plan is put into effect?

~~~

## question 8

Trump's victory, as per Malcolm Nance, was no less "won with the aid of Americans who had turned on their own values." How have the American pro-Trump voters turned on their values? What values is Nance referring to?

~~~

~~~

## question 9

Nance writes that Trump is pulling America down for monetary gain along with "the American Goebbels." Who are the figures that he is referring to? What are the evidences that link them to Trump's alleged agenda?

~~~

## question 10

"The American Goebbels," that's what Nance calls Trump's pro-Moscow team. Why did he call them so? What exactly do they do to bring America down?

~~~

# question 11

Nance calls Trump a malignant narcissist whose idiocy will bring America down. What instances is Nance speaking of? Which of Trump's actions merit the label 'idiocy'?

## question 12

Trump's family was also included by Nance in his exposé. Who among his family members are part of this alleged pro-Moscow movement?

~~~

# question 13

To write this comprehensive exposé, Nance researched government documents and conducted interviews. Which documents did Nance spotlight in his book? Who did he interview for this exposé?

~~~

## question 14

According to Nance, Putin seeks to overthrow a number of democratic institutions and international alliances. Which international alliances does Putin seek to overthrow? What American democratic institutions are included in Putin's grand plan?

## question 15

Putin has employed active measures to exploit the existing divisions within the American government. What does Nance mean with "active measures"? Explain.

## question 16

*Net Galley* describes Malcolm Nance's *The Plot to Destroy Democracy: How Putin and His Spies Are Undermining America and Dismantling the West* "revelatory, insightful and shocking." Nance has exposed many secrets between the White House and Kremlin. What is most shocking to you?

~ ~ ~

~~~

## question 17

*Kirkus Reviews* says that Nance's book "convincing and alarming." Which among Nance's numerous claims is the most convincing? Explain your answer.

~~~

## question 18

*Publishers Weekly* depict Nance's book as an "unconvincing exaggeration of genuine misconduct into cartoonish supervillainy". Why did *Publishers Weekly* compare Nance's book into a "cartoonish supervillainy"?

~~~

## question 19

*Philadelphia* quotes Joy Reid in their article on Malcolm Nance. Reid states "Malcolm was predicting all of the events we're seeing now in the summer of 2016." What events did Nance predict in 2016 that's happening now?

## question 20

In an article in *Philadelphia,* actor Mark Hamill calls Malcolm Nance "the real deal." How has Nance merited this label? Why is Malcolm Nance called by *Philadelphia* "the new hero of resistance?

# Introducing the Author

**M**ALCOLM WRIGHTSON NANCE IS A WELL-KNOWN voice on counterterrorism and military intelligence. He has been interviewed in NBC and in the films *Torturing Democracy* (2008), *Dirty Wars* (2013) and *Trump: The Kremlin Candidate* (2017). Malcolm Nance was born in Philadelphia. He graduated from West Catholic Boys High School and studied foreign languages at South Philadelphia High School. He served in the U.S. Navy for twenty years. His received a number of military decorations for his exceptional service from 1981 to 2001. He took part in the combat operations after the 1983 Beirut barracks bombings. In 1986, he was involved in the 1986 United States bombing of Libya. He also served during Operation Praying Mantis on USS Wainwright. He was aboard the Iranian missile boat Joshan and he witnessed its sinking. During the Gulf War, he served on USS Tripoli and assisted during the Bosnia air strike.

Malcolm Nance was a U.S. Navy specialist in Naval Cryptology. His involvement in counter-terrorism, intelligence and combat operations garnered him expertise in these fields. During his active service in the military, he became an instructor in wartime and peacetime SERE, this stands for Survival, Evasion, Resistance and Escape. He trained Navy and Marine Corps pilots and aircrew how to survive in the chance that they are held as prisoners of war. Nance also initiated a new course of instruction on Advanced Terrorism, Abduction and Hostage Survival.

After his service in the Navy, he retired and studied an online degree from New York's Excelsior College. In 2001, he founded an intelligence support company - Special Readiness Services International (SRSI). Nance acted as a first responder at the crash site of American Airlines Flight 77 that crashed into the Pentagon on the fateful day of September 11, 2011. He helped organize the rescue and recovery of victims.

Nance is frequently tapped as an intelligence consultant and security contractor in Iraq,

Afghanistan, the UAE and North Africa. In 2005-2007, he was a visiting instructor on counterterrorism in Macquarie University's Centre on Policing, Intelligence and Counter-terrorism (PICT) in Sydney. He has also taught in Victoria University of Wellington in New Zealand. Nance founded Terror Asymmetrics Project on Strategy, Tactics and Radical Ideologies, which analyzes counterterrorism. He is a member of International Spy Museum's advisory board of directors in Washington D.C.

In 2007, Nance wrote an article in the blog *Small Wars Journal*. He criticized waterboarding and called it "torture... period." This articles was republished in the *Pentagon Early Bird*. This is the first credible description of SERE torture technique. The U.S. Congress summoned Nance to testify about the use of enhanced interrogation techniques.

He began researching on the history of the Soviet Union and the KGB. He also analyzed Middle East terrorism and sovereign nations linked to the Russian Federation. His work in the civilian intelligence arena led him to publish bestselling books. His published works are *An End to Al-Qaeda, Terrorist Recognition Handbook, Defeating ISIS, The Plot to Hack America, Hacking ISIS* and *The Plot to Destroy Democracy*.

# Fireside Questions

*"What would you do?"*

**Tip:** These questions can be a fun exercise as it spurs creativity among the readers by allowing alternate scene endings and "if this was you" questions.

## question 21

Malcolm Nance graduated from West Catholic Boys High School and studied foreign languages at South Philadelphia High School. Which foreign languages did Malcolm Nance study? How did his knowledge on foreign languages help his career as an intelligence office?

## question 22

During his active service in the U.S. Navy, he was part of many operations. In one instance, he was aboard a sinking Iranian missile boat. What was the name of the Iranian missile boat? What was his assignment in Iran?

## question 23

On the fateful day of September 11, 2011, Nance witnessed how American Airlines Flight 77 that crashed into the Pentagon. How did he respond in the crash?

~~~

## question 24

Malcolm Nance became an instructor in wartime and peacetime SERE. What does SERE stand for? And what did course Nance initiate in the U.S. Navy?

## question 25

The U.S. Congress summoned Nance to testify. Why did the Congress ask Nance's knowledge on enhanced interrogation techniques? What article instigated this request?

## question 26

Rachel Maddow, the host of MSNBC's prime-time tent-pole program, says in an interview that Nance was the only one "willing to stick his neck out." If you were Malcolm Nance, will you "stick your neck out" so the American public can find out the truth?

~~~

## question 27

Nance criticized waterboarding in an article he wrote in the blog *Small Wars Journal*. Is it wise nowadays to use online platforms to expose such information? Will you do the same if given the knowledge Nance has?

~~~

## question 28

*Publishers Weekly* called Nance's book an "unconvincing exaggeration of genuine misconduct into cartoonish supervillainy". If you were Malcolm Nance, how will you react to this review?

~~~

## question 29

Nance acted as a first responder at the crash site of American Airlines Flight 77. How would you respond when you witness a crash of the same scale as that in the Pentagon?

~~~

## question 30

Nance's comprehensive research on the Soviet Union and the KGB gave birth to his bestselling books. Russia is one giant to battle for Malcolm Nance. Given the immensity of Russian power, will you write against this superpower in public, like Nance did?

~ ~ ~

# Quiz Questions

*"Ready to Announce the Winners?"*

**Tip:** Create a leaderboard and track scores to see who gets the most correct answers. Winners required. Prizes optional.

~~~

## quiz question 1

What year was the first publication of *The Plot to Destroy Democracy*?

~~~

## quiz question 2

According to Nance, who is the key person in forging America into a pro-Moscow movement?

## quiz question 3

What activity does Nance call "torture"?

## quiz question 4

Where did Malcolm Nance earn his online degree?

~ ~ ~

## quiz question 5

**True or False:** According to Nance, Vladimir Putin is the real victor when Donald Trump won the 2016 presidential elections.

## quiz question 6

**True or False:** Nance strongly suggest that Russia wants to destroy the international alliance ASEAN.

## quiz question 7

**True or False:** Nance writes that Trump is pulling America down for monetary gain along with "the American Goebbels."

~~~

## quiz question 8

Malcolm Nance served aboard USS Wainwright during Operation _____.

~~~

## quiz question 9

Malcolm Nance specializes in _____.

~~~

## quiz question 10

**True or False:** Malcolm Nance graduated from West Catholic Boys High School.

~~~

## quiz question 11

**True or False:** Nance authored the book *An End to Al-Qaeda.*

# quiz question 12

**True or False:** Nance witnessed American Airlines Flight 77's crash into the Twin Towers on September 11, 2011

# Quiz Answers

1.   2018
2.   Steve Brannon
3.   Waterboarding
4.   New York's Excelsior College
5.   True
6.   False
7.   True
8.   Praying Mantis
9.   Cryptology
10.  True
11.  True
12.  False

# Ways to Continue Your Reading

EVERY month, our team runs through a wide selection of books to pick the best titles for readers and reading groups, and promotes these titles to our thousands of readers – sometimes with free downloads, sale dates, and additional brochures.

### Click here to sign up for these benefits.

**If you have not yet read the original work or would like to read it again, you can** purchase the original book here.

# On the Next Page...

If you found this book helpful to your discussions and rate it a 4 or 5, please write us a review on the next page.

*Any* length would be fine but we'd appreciate hearing you more! We'd be very encouraged.

**Till next time,**

**BookHabits**

*"Loving Books is Actually a Habit"*

CPSIA information can be obtained
at www.ICGtesting.com
Printed in the USA
BVHW031656110219
539954BV00007B/935/P

9 781388 338336